CINCINNATI UNION TERMINAL

Originally published in 1933 by the Cincinnati Chamber of Congress
to celebrate the dedication of Cincinnati Union Terminal.
This facsimile edition is published by

COMMONWEALTH BOOK COMPANY
St. Martin, Ohio

ISBN: 978-1-948986-43-4

Foreword...

THIS volume commemorates the dedication to public service of a great temple of transportation.

The Cincinnati Union Terminal has come into being, a perfectly coordinated instrument for the swift dispatch and acceleration of passenger, freight, express and postal traffic. The long, tortuous course of its progress from inception to completion constitutes one of the finest epics in American industrial achievement. Consecrated to public use and the promotion of the general welfare, the terminal becomes a monumental tribute to the idealism, the artistry and the indomitable courage of the men responsible for its conception and creation.

It constitutes the virile, vibrant challenge of American railroads to the bogey of obsolescence and decay. Unfettered by harsh, unfair, repressive and destructive governmental regulation, railroad equipment and operation will quickly reflect the beauty and efficiency of the Cincinnati Terminal. The railroad will continue to be the bulwark of transportation and a mighty factor in our national destiny.

CINCINNATI UNION TERMINAL
DEDICATED
MARCH 31, 1933

CINCINNATI'S TERMINAL, IN WHICH STRUCTURAL MASSIVENESS AND ARCHITECTURAL GRANDEUR GREET THE EYE

WHEN NIGHT SHADOWS THE PLAZA AND THE FRONT OF THE GREAT EDIFICE BECOMES A RADIANT DISC OF LIGHT

IMPOSING BY DAY . . MAGNIFICENT BY NIGHT . . THE
UNION TERMINAL BUILDING HAS ENDURING APPEAL

ANGULAR MONOTONY IS BROKEN BY THE GRACEFUL
CURVES OF BOULEVARD LANES AND VEHICULAR DRIVES

RAMPS OF GENEROUS WIDTH AND EASY GRADE
PROVIDE ENTRANCE FOR CABS AND FOR BUSSES

PASSENGERS UNLOADED, THE CABS PROCEED OUT FRONT,
WHILE THEIR FARES ENTER STATION BY STEPS OR RAMP

THROUGH SWINGING DOORS OF AN IMPOSING EN-
TRANCE-WAY, PASSENGERS ENTER MAIN CONCOURSE

RAMPS FOR OUTGOING VEHICLES . . MOTOR
COACHES ON THE RIGHT, CABS ON THE LEFT

THE GREAT WINDOWED FRONT CASTS MIRRORED LIGHT
UPON THE BALCONY, WHICH ROOFS ATTRACTIVE SHOPS

QUICK ACCESS TO THE CITY IS AFFORDED THE
TRAVELER .. JUST BEYOND THIS EFFECTIVE PORTAL

THE HISTORY OF AMERICAN TRANSPORTATION FROM THE EARLY DOG TRAVOIS OF THE INDIAN TO THE AIR CRUISER OF THE PRESENT TIME, FORMS THE BACKGROUND THEME. THE MIDDLE BACKGROUND PRESENTS THE COVERED WAGON OF THE '40'S, THE EARLY EFFORTS OF STEAM TRANSPORTATION AND THE MODERN MOGUL ENGINE. THE FERRYBOAT OF YESTERYEAR AND THE OCEAN GREYHOUND OF TODAY COMPLETE THE PORTRAIT SCENE OF A CITY PHANTASTIQUE.

LEFT OR SOUTH MURAL IN THE MAIN CONCOURSE

IN THE FOREGROUND, ANOTHER STORY IS TOLD—THE ADVANCE OF CIVILIZATION FROM THE PROUD BLACKFEET THROUGH THE AGE OF THE HARDY PIONEER. A NEW ERA DAWNS WITH THE COMING OF THE RAILROAD BUILDER AND CARRIES ON TO THE AGE OF STEEL.

RIGHT OR NORTH MURAL IN THE MAIN CONCOURSE

THE GROWTH OF CINCINNATI, IS THE EPIC UNFOLDED IN THREE SYMBOLICAL EXPRESSIONS. THE UPPER BACKGROUND PORTRAYS THE ADVANCING DESIGN OF THE RIVER BOAT AND ENDS WITH THE AEROPLANE AS IT WINGS ITS WAY OVER THE CINCINNATI OF TOMORROW. THE LOWER BACKGROUND REPEATS THE STORY, AS THE EPIC MOVES FROM THE FIRST CABIN ON THE OHIO TO THE EARLY SETTLEMENT, THENCE TO THE LATER RURAL LIFE AND INTO THE CINCINNATI OF TODAY.

THE STORY IS AGAIN REPEATED IN A THIRD EXPRESSION—MAN. THE PERIOD OF THE SCOUT AND SOLDIER IN THE DAYS OF FORT WASHINGTON ENDS AS GENERAL ST. CLAIR RENAMES LOSANTIVILLE. THE FARMER AND BRIDGE-BUILDER MOVE ON THROUGH THE PICTURESQUE RIVER AGE OF THE NEGRO AND CAPTAIN TO THE WORKERS IN INDUSTRY—BUILDERS OF CITIES.

PARENTS WILL EXPERIENCE DIFFICULTY IN COAXING
THEIR KIDDIES OUT OF THIS APPEALING TOY SHOP

THE NEWS REEL'S THE THING FOR TEDIOUS "BETWEEN-TRAINS" TIME

A LOVELY LITTLE THEATRE .. WITH COMFORTABLE OPERA CHAIRS AND A REAL PLAYHOUSE ATMOSPHERE

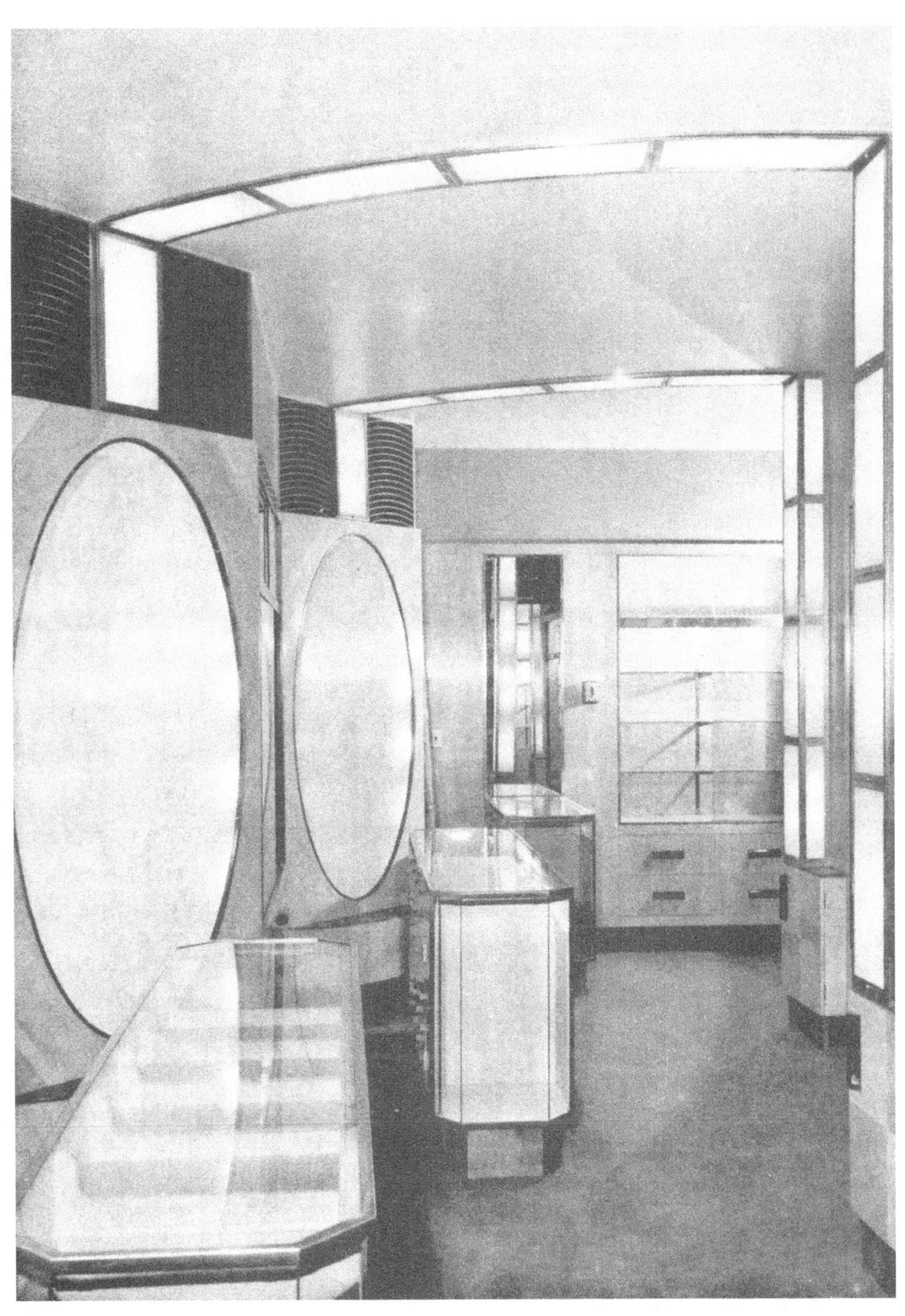

THE WOMEN'S SHOP, WHERE LOST OR FORGOTTEN
ARTICLES OF DRESS OR TOILET MAY BE REPLACED

VISITORS ARE CAPTIVATED BY THE ROOKWOOD TEA ROOM. IT IS . . WELL, A ROOKWOOD CREATION

A MODEL OF SMARTNESS AND COMPLETENESS IN APPOINTMENTS . . . IS THE MEN'S SHOP

ALONG NORTH ROTUNDA WALL BETWEEN MARBLE
LIGHTING COLUMNS, ARE THE TICKET WINDOWS

PATHWAYS PERMANENTLY MARKED IN TERRAZZO
FLOORS SUGGEST THE NORMAL TRAFFIC ARTERIES

FROM CENTER OF MAIN CONCOURSE, ALL PRINCIPAL
FACILITIES ARE SEEN IN THEIR PROPER RELATIONSHIP

THE POWER OF SUGGESTION IS STRONG AS ONE ENTERS RESTAURANT CORRIDOR FROM MAIN CONCOURSE

THE SANDWICH SHOP WITH ITS HORSESHOE TABLES
WAS DESIGNED TO MEET QUICK SERVICE NEEDS

ATTRACTIVE TABLES AND CHAIRS OF ALUMINUM
WEIGHT ARE FEATURES OF THE DINING ROOM

THE MIRRORS OF THE DINING ROOM CREATE THE
PLEASING ILLUSION OF A GARDEN OF FERNS

THE MAIN DINING ROOM, WITH ITS DISTINCTIVE
CURVED BALCONY, WINS APPROVAL ON SIGHT

STAINLESS, RUST-RESISTING METALS IN THIS KITCHEN
EQUIPMENT MAKE FOR STRICT CLEANLINESS

HUGE KETTLES, AUTOMATIC STEAMERS PLACED ON
SANITARY DRAIN PANS AND AGAINST TILED WALLS

GORGEOUS PRIVATE DINING ROOMS ON THE
ELASTIC PLAN ARE PROVIDED ON THE UPPER FLOOR

ONE SECTION OF A PRIVATE DINING ROOM...
ARRANGED TO COMFORTABLY SEAT TEN GUESTS

AN INSTANCE OF MODERNISM AS APPLIED TO THE
DECORATIVE DESIGN OF THE WOMEN'S LOUNGE

THE TELEPHONE BOOTHS LEAVE NOTHING TO BE DESIR-
ED IN THE MATTER OF GOOD TASTE AND CONVENIENCE

AN ARTISTIC APPLICATION OF INDIRECT LIGHTING
FOR READERS, IS A FEATURE OF THE WOMEN'S ROOM

A MAN'S ROOM . . WITH COMPLETE SERVICES
SO NECESSARY TO MASCULINITY, AT HAND

ELEGANCE, DIGNITY AND REFINEMENT CONSTITUTE
THE ENTRANCE THEME TO THE PRESIDENT'S OFFICE

WHERE OFFICE FURNISHINGS AND EQUIPMENT
HAVE ANTICIPATED THE PRESIDENT'S REQUIREMENTS

ADJACENT TO THE EXECUTIVE SUITE ARE THE CORRECTLY APPOINTED QUARTERS OF THE SECRETARY

WARMTH IS LENT TO COLD BUSINESS CONFERENCE IN
THE DIRECTORS' ROOM ADJOINING THE EXECUTIVE SUITE

SOLUTION TO VEXATIOUS TERMINAL COMPANY PROBLEMS WILL BE ATTAINED AT THIS DIRECTORS' TABLE

MANY CONVENIENCES ARE INCORPORATED WITHIN THE
GROUP OF ROOMS SURROUNDING THE CHECKING LOBBY

WHEN BRUSHED WITH SOFT LIGHT FROM WITHIN, THE GREAT SWEEP OF THE ROTUNDA FRONT COMPELS ADMIRATION

LEATHER COVERED LOUNGING CHAIRS, IN NON-CONVENTIONAL GROUPS, ARE INTERSPERSED BETWEEN TRAIN GATES

THE CONDUCTOR'S VISA IS A FOCAL POINT IN THIS MOSAIC
PANELED CONCOURSE, DISTINGUISHED FOR ARTISTIC BEAUTY

TIME TRAVELS ON . . . A MOSAIC MAP OF THE UNITED
STATES UPON WHICH TIME BOUNDARIES ARE DESIGNATED

FINE balance of industry, commerce and culture is found in Cincinnati. It is natural, then, that the terminal should reflect this symmetry. Fourteen leading industries are portrayed by silhouette mosaic panels on the walls of the train concourse.

Delicate pigments, used in mural paintings, are easily destroyed by impurities in the atmosphere. For this reason, the more practical silhouette mosaic medium was chosen and has never before been employed on so large a scale, or to depict such subjects as machinery.

One who creates and paints cartoons for mosaics is limited in his expression to broad decorative effects by simplification of design. He must retain all color shades and yet make the setting of the mosaic not too intricate.

These mosaic presentations of Industrial Cincinnati give to the city a new art treasure.

CERAMICS, an industry as old as civilization, plays a dual role, by occupying an equally important position in both the industrial and cultural life of Cincinnati.

WINOLD REISS, artist, who created the cartoons for the terminal mosaics, reproduced on the succeeding pages, was kind enough to contribute the cover design for this book.

THE MANUFACTURE OF PIANOS

QUITE NATURALLY A CITY NOTED FOR ITS MUSICAL TRADITIONS AND SKILLED CRAFTSMEN, EARLY BECAME A PIONEER IN THE MANUFACTURE OF PIANOS

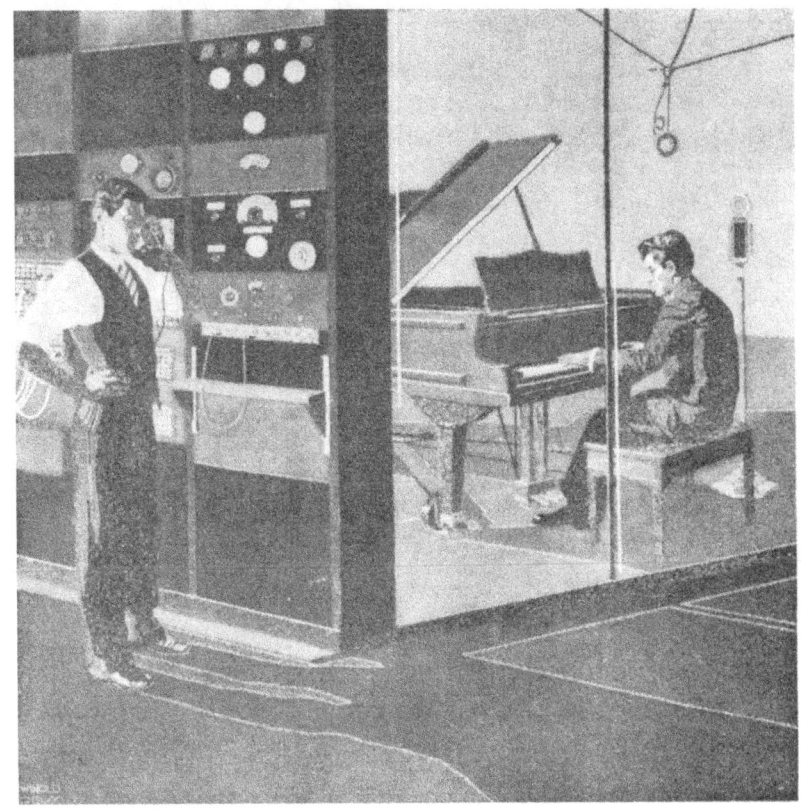

RADIO BROADCASTING AND MANUFACTURE

AMERICA'S LATEST MAJOR INDUSTRY IS REPRESENTED IN CINCINNATI BY THE MOST POWERFUL BROADCASTING STATION NOW IN EXISTENCE

ROOFING AND SHINGLES

IN ONE OF THE WORLD'S LARGEST PAPER PRODUCING DISTRICTS, THE LOCATION OF PLANTS TO MANUFACTURE ROOFING AND COMPOSITION SHINGLES . . WAS A LOGICAL SEQUENCE

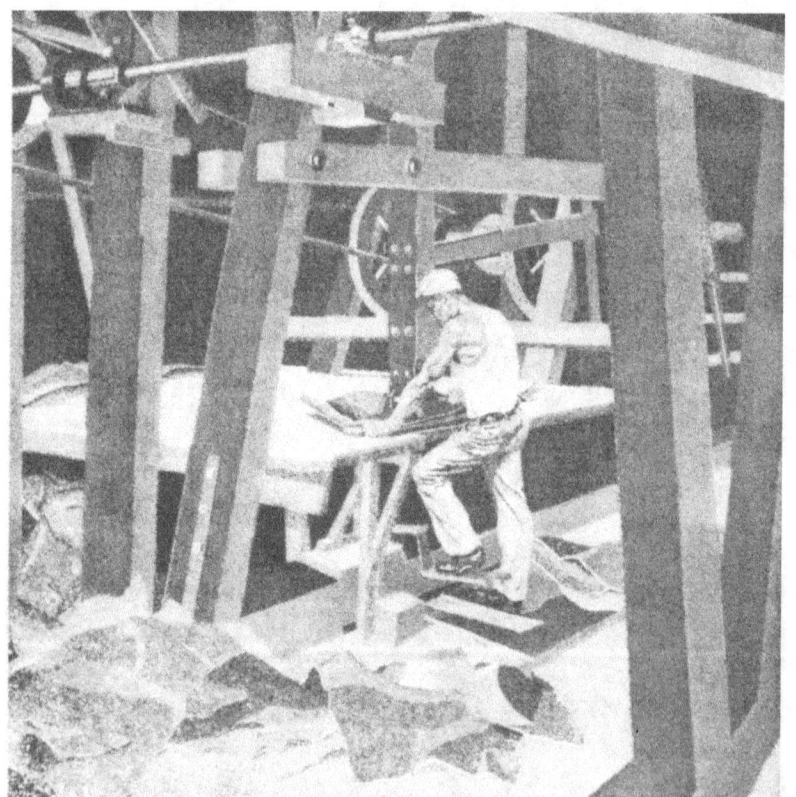

LEATHER AND TANNING

TANNING OF LEATHER . . ONE OF THE OLDER INDUSTRIES IN WHICH CINCINNATI EXCELLED . . CONTINUES TO PLAY A LEADING PART IN THE CITY'S INDUSTRIAL LIFE

AEROPLANES AND PARTS

FORESIGHT OF CITY OFFICIALS IN RESERVING ACREAGE AT THE MUNICIPAL AIRPORT FOR AIRCRAFT MANUFACTURE, FACILITATED THE ESTABLISHMENT OF THIS INDUSTRY IN CINCINNATI

INKS . . PRINTING AND WRITING

TREMENDOUS REQUIREMENTS OF THE FOURTH LARGEST PRINTING AND PUBLISHING CENTER IN THE COUNTRY BROUGHT RELATED INDUSTRIES INTO EQUAL PROMINENCE

LAUNDRY MACHINERY

THE TRANSFER OF HOME DRUDGERY TO CENTRALIZED MASS PRODUCTION, DEMANDED EQUIPMENT BEST DEVELOPED IN A GREAT FOUNDRY AND MACHINE SHOP CENTER

MACHINE TOOLS

AN INTERNATIONAL INDUSTRY HAS GIVEN TO CINCINNATI THE DISTINCTION OF BEING "THE MACHINE TOOL CENTER OF THE WORLD"

SOAP MANUFACTURE

FOR GENERATIONS THIS HAS BEEN THE CITY'S MOST PROMINENT INDUSTRY. CINCINNATI IS TODAY ONE OF THE WORLD'S CHIEF SOAP-PRODUCING CENTERS

SHEET STEEL

WITHIN THE CINCINNATI INDUSTRIAL AREA TWO GREAT ROLLING MILLS ADEQUATELY MEET THE REQUIREMENTS OF THE STEEL AGE

FOUNDRY AND MACHINE SHOP PRODUCTS

THIS IS A BASIC INDUSTRY OF ANY GREAT MACHINERY CENTER, AND, COMBINED WITH THE MANUFACTURE OF MACHINE TOOLS .. IT IS CINCINNATI'S LEADING INDUSTRY IN THE VALUE OF PRODUCTION

PRINTING, PUBLISHING AND LITHOGRAPHING

SKILLED CRAFTSMEN, THE CITY'S PROXIMITY TO RAW MATERIALS, AND LOW DISTRIBUTION COSTS HAVE MADE THIS INDUSTRY THIRD IN RANK IN THE CITY OF CINCINNATI

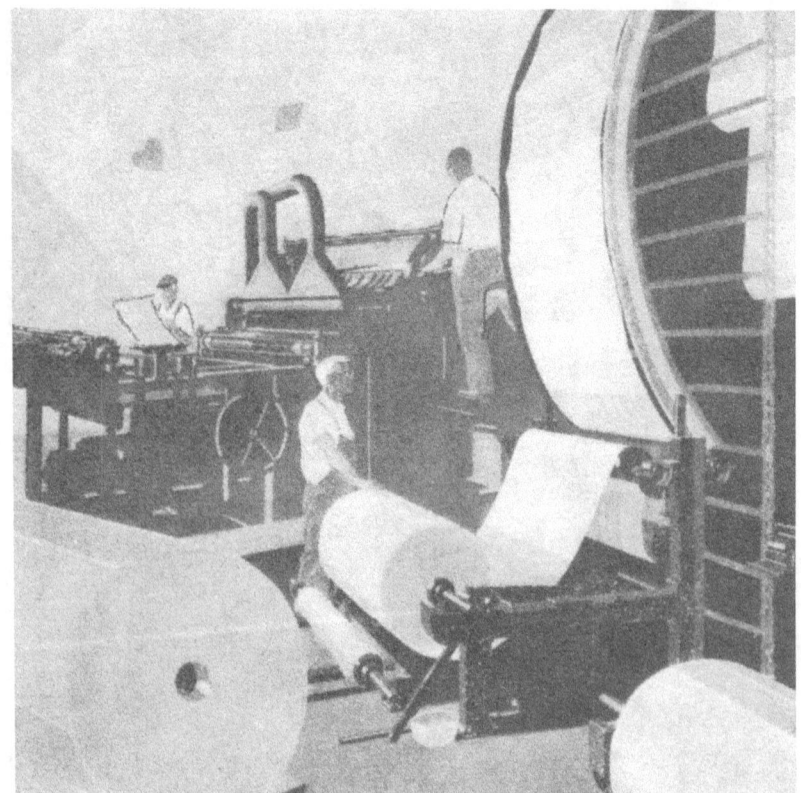

DRUGS AND CHEMICALS

DRUGS AND CHEMICALS HAVE BEEN PRODUCED IN CINCINNATI FOR OVER 100 YEARS, RESULTING IN THE ESTABLISHMENT OF LARGE ACID PHOSPHATE PLANTS SUPPLYING THE INDUSTRIAL AND AGRICULTURAL MARKETS

MEAT PACKING AND SLAUGHTERING

FROM THE VERY BEGINNING, MEAT PACKING AND SLAUGHTERING HAS REMAINED THE LARGEST SINGLE INDUSTRY, AND MATERIALLY AIDED TRADE WITH THE SOUTH AND SOUTHWEST

TWO EQUALLY ERROR-PROOF WAYS THAT LEAD FROM
THE TRAIN CONCOURSE TO THE TRAIN PLATFORMS

LIKE THE BRIDGE OF A SHIP, THE INTERLOCKING TOWER
PERMITS SAFE GUIDANCE FOR THE GREAT STEEL GIANTS

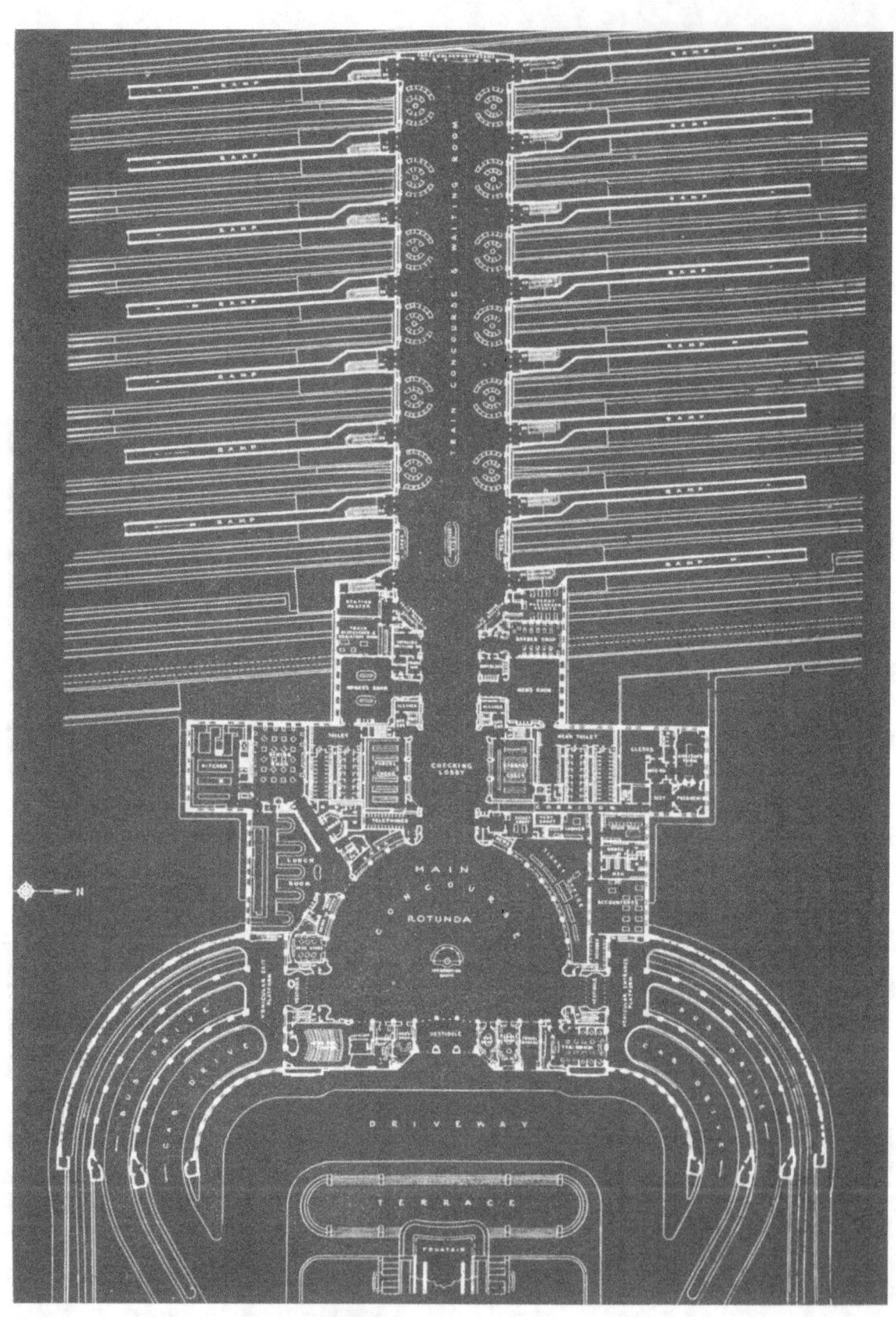

MAIN FLOOR PLAN OF THE STATION BUILDING,
DRAWN BY FELLHEIMER & WAGNER, ARCHITECTS

THE CINCINNATI UNION TERMINAL DEVELOPMENT
INCLUDING ALL OF THE FIVE TRAIN APPROACHES

APPROACH FROM SOUTHERN BRIDGE..PASSENGER CONNECTION TO LEFT, FREIGHT TO RIGHT. THE SOUTH-WEST APPROACH PASSES UNDER THIS SOUTHERN CONNECTION

THE SOUTH-EAST CONNECTION IS USED BY THE L. & N. AND C. & O. TRAINS FROM THE SOUTH

THE SOUTH-WEST CONNECTION IS USED BY TRAINS OF THE B. & O. AND THE BIG FOUR FROM THE WEST

C. & O. OF INDIANA TRAINS ENTER VIA THE WESTERN HILLS, THENCE OVER THIS ELEVATED STRUCTURE, PASSENGER TO THE RIGHT AND FREIGHT TO THE LEFT

THE SOUTH-WEST AND SOUTH-EAST CONNECTIONS MEET STATION TRACKS AT THIS POINT .. WHERE STANDS SIGNAL BRIDGE, WHICH CONTROLS THEIR ENTRANCE

SIGNAL BRIDGE WHICH CONTROLS ENTRANCE TO
STATION FOR TRAINS APPROACHING FROM NORTH

THE NORTHERN APPROACH USED BY THE PENNSYLVANIA
AND N. & W., ALSO THE BIG FOUR AND B. & O.

SOUTHERN ELEVATION OF MAIL HANDLING BUILDING, AND PASSAGE-WAY COMMUNICATION WITH STATION

COMPLETE MAIL HANDLING UNIT FROM RECEIVING PLATFORMS TO THE NEW U. S. POST OFFICE

THE LATEST FACILITIES FOR EFFICIENT MAIL HANDLING ARE INCORPORATED IN THIS BUILDING

MODERN TREATMENT IN DETAIL OF THE EAST
ENTRANCE TO THE RAILWAY EXPRESS BUILDING

AMPLE SPACE AND ADEQUATE FACILITIES ARE HERE
PROVIDED FOR THE HANDLING OF RAILWAY EXPRESS

LOADING PLATFORMS THAT MEET A GREAT CITY'S
EXPRESSAGE NEEDS FOR TODAY AND TOMORROW

THE MAJOR GROUP . . EXPRESS, MAIL HANDLING
AND STATION . . IN A UNIQUE PERSPECTIVE

UTILITY GROUP SOUTH OF THE VIADUCT . . WATER TOWER, COAL TIPPLE AND YARD SERVICE BUILDING

THE COMPLETE UTILITY GROUP, LOCATED AT THE NORTH END OF THE TERMINAL DEVELOPMENT

SPANNING SPRING GROVE AVENUE, THIS GREAT ARCH
SUPPORTS UPPER LEVEL OF WESTERN HILLS VIADUCT

NEAR AND DISTANT VIEWS OF THE SPRING GROVE
ARCH REVEAL STRENGTH AND IMPLICIT BEAUTY

FROM THE WESTERN PLAZA, TEN LANES OF TRAFFIC TO
UPPER AND LOWER DECKS OF WESTERN HILLS VIADUCT

LOOKING ACROSS MILL CREEK . . THE POPULOUS
WESTERN HILLS, NOW BEING SERVED BY THIS VIADUCT

MILL CREEK ARCH . . TWO STUDIES IN WHICH CHARM
AND SIMPLICITY OF DESIGN ACCOMPANY UTILITY

WEST FROM SPRING GROVE AVENUE .. A BRILLIANTLY
ILLUMINATED SURFACE APPEALING TO MOTORISTS

AS THE BROAD WESTERN APPROACH APPEARS
WHEN NIGHT CANOPIES THE MILL CREEK VALLEY

FOCUSED WEST THE CAMERA DISCOVERS
TWO CURVES .. A MYRIAD OF LIGHTS

BROKEN FLIGHTS OF EASY STEPS COM-
MUNICATE WITH THE UPPER DECK

LIGHT THAT ILLUMINATES WITHOUT BLINDING
MAKES NIGHT AS SAFE AS DAY ON THE VIADUCT

MODERN ENGINEERING ACCOMPLISHMENT IN TRAFFIC ROUTING AT THE WESTERN LOWER LEVEL EXITS

BEAUTY, SIMPLICITY AND UTILITY IN TREATMENT OF THE LIGHTING COLUMNS

THE IMPRESSIVE EASTERN APPROACH OF THE VIADUCT'S LOWER LEVEL BY NIGHT

THE FULL SPAN OF THE BOW-SHAPED VIADUCT . . A
VALLEY OF INDUSTRY . . RESIDENTIAL HILLS BEYOND

STRENGTH AND ARTISTRY ARE HAPPILY UNITED IN
THE PLEASING COMPOSITION OF MILL CREEK ARCH

MODERN STRUCTURAL DESIGN, SPARTAN SIMPLICITY.. CHARACTERISTIC THROUGHOUT THE VIADUCT

THE LOFTY BOILER HOUSE CHIMNEY IS VISIBLE
FROM ALL POINTS WITHIN THE TERMINAL AREA

THE UTILITY GROUP, WITH ITS LEAD-IN TRACKS
PASSING UNDER THE WESTERN HILLS VIADUCT

THE ENGINE HOUSE . . WHERE LOCOMOTIVE IN-
SPECTION AND REPAIRS ARE MADE AFTER EACH RUN

TURN TABLE WAITING TO RECEIVE LOCOMOTIVE FROM ENGINE HOUSE

BACKED ONTO TURN TABLE AFTER RECONDITIONING

NOW, COMING OFF THE TURN TABLE READY TO RESUME THE REGULAR RUN

THE CENTRAL UNION DEPOT—1884-1933

THE PENNSYLVANIA STATION—1880-1933

THE OLD FOURTH STREET STATION

INTERIOR OF OLD CENTRAL UNION DEPOT

THE OLD COURT STREET STATION

INTERIOR OF OLD PENNSYLVANIA STATION

C. H. & D. DEPOT 1859-1933.

STATIONS REPLACED BY THE NEW UNION TERMINAL

T. C. POWELL
CHRMN. COM. OF EXECUTIVES
THE CINCINNATI RAILWAYS
1912-1918

H. A. WORCESTER
CHRMN. COM. OF EXECUTIVES
THE CINCINNATI RAILWAYS
1918-1927

C. A. WILSON
CONSULTING ENGINEER
1912-1927

F. L. STUART
CHRMN. ENGINEERS' COM.
ON TERMINAL MATTERS
1913-1916

B. V. SOMMERVILLE
MEMBER ENGINEERS' COMMITTEE
1913-1916

A FEW OF THE MANY MEN WHO DEVELOPED EARLIER
STUDIES OF THE CINCINNATI UNION TERMINAL PROJECT

MURRAY SEASONGOOD
MAYOR

C. O. SHERRILL
CITY MANAGER

JOHN D. ELLIS
CITY SOLICITOR

CHARLES O. ROSE
CHAIRMAN, FINANCE COMMITTEE

LOUIS B. BLAKEMORE
CLERK OF COUNCIL

H. F. SHIPLEY
HIGHWAY ENGINEER

L. SEGOE
CITY PLANNING COM'N ENG'R

CITY OF CINCINNATI OFFICIALS AT THE TIME OF
THE INAUGURATION OF THE TERMINAL PROJECT

COL. H. M. WAITE
CHIEF ENGINEER FOR THE
CINCINNATI UNION TERMINAL CO.

SPECIAL ENGINEERING STAFF. FRONT ROW, LEFT TO RIGHT. H. E. ROUSE, W. R. KELLOGG, J. B. SULLIVAN, H. F. WHITEHEAD, E. W. CLARK, PUSEY JONES, PETER BERG, S. A. McGAVERN: REAR ROW: L. A. GILLETT, RODGER BEAR, EDGAR D. TYLER, H. G. CHAPMAN, A. H. SULLIVAN, GEO. P. STOWITTS, COL. H. M. WAITE, F. C. BUSSEY, EDISON BROCK, J. E. BRAND, E. W. WILLING, E. ROBERTS, AND G. H. WELLS. C. A. WILSON WAS NOT PRESENT WHEN PICTURE WAS MADE.

ALFRED T. FELLHEIMER
ARCHITECT

A. M. STEWART
GENERAL CONTRACTOR

STEWARD WAGNER
ARCHITECT

WINOLD REISS
ARTIST

Tons of earth were moved, and tons
    Of steel, of iron, were melted white,
And ribbon rails were forged and laid;
    Men and machines toiled day and night.

More wood, more stone and marble, too,
    Swing arms, swing tools, in loud refrain—
Concrete poured in from dippers huge;
    And thus they strove, with brawn and brain.

Neat spandrels, borders, etched designs,
    And lovely patterns formed in brass,
All laced and woven intricate
    With tiny bits of colored glass.

'Til all's complete, each wall, each arch,
    Each atom small, each heavy beam
In perfect place, composite, whole,
    This giant thing built from a dream.

Hewed out, fine-wrought, below, above,
    This Palace high of Transportation—
Where turn the wheels of man, of time,
    In pageantry . . . . Civilization.

                —Donna Harkness.

PICTURESQUE BALD KNOB . . MASSIVE HILL TO THE
WEST . . A CONVENIENT SOURCE OF FILL MATERIAL

FILLING AND GRADING MILL CREEK VALLEY WAS
A MAJOR FEATURE OF THIS GIGANTIC TASK

"TONS OF EARTH WERE MOVED,—"

FOUNDATIONS OF ALL TERMINAL BUILDINGS REST
ON SPECIALLY-MADE PILES FILLED WITH CONCRETE

MUCH PRELIMINARY WORK HAD TO BE ACCOMPLISHED BEFORE BUILDING OPERATIONS BEGAN

HALF A MILLION TONS OF CONCRETE WERE MIXED
IN TRANSIT, AND DELIVERED BY RAIL AND TRUCK

"CONCRETE POURED IN FROM DIPPERS HUGE"

THIS MASTERPIECE OF STEEL FRAME WORK
SUSTAINS THE GREAT ROTUNDA DOME

WHEN THE BOILER HOUSE WAS A SKELETON
OF STEEL BESIDE A FINISHED CHIMNEY

SKILLED AND FEARLESS MASTERS OF MANY
CRAFTS TOILED ON THIS COLOSSAL PROJECT

"—AND TONS OF STEEL, OF IRON,—"

SWINGING SIXTY-TON GIRDERS INTO POSITION
WAS A MERE INCIDENT IN THE DAY'S WORK

SOME OF THE STRUCTURAL BEAMS REQUIRED
BY THIS DEVELOPMENT MEASURED 145 FEET

TRAFFIC PROCEEDED AS USUAL WHILE GIRDERS OF ENOR-
MOUS WEIGHT WERE EASED ABOUT OVERHEAD

"EACH ATOM SMALL, EACH HEAVY BEAM"

THE CONSTRUCTION OF FORTY-FIVE MILES OF TERMINAL TRACKS REQUIRED MUCH MATERIAL

TIES AND RAILS CAME IN CARLOADS

CREWS OF WORKMEN ON THE JOB

MAZE OF TRACKAGE WHERE AUTOMATIC SWITCHES CLICK AND SIGNAL LIGHTS FLASH ON AND OFF

"AND RIBBON RAILS WERE FORGED AND LAID"

FACTS AND FIGURES
CINCINNATI UNION TERMINAL

Work started August, 1929 — completed March 31, 1933.

Total cost $41,000,000, including purchase of ground and readjusting railroad facilities.

Area — 287 acres.

5,663,065 cubic yards of fill material used.

94 miles of track laid.

224,534 cubic yards of concrete poured, not including 100,500 square yards of paving.

22 distinct buildings constructed.

8,250,000 bricks used.

45,421 net tons of steel used in bridge and building construction.

More than 300 separate contracts negotiated.

Western Hills Viaduct, costing $3,500,000, built by the Cincinnati Union Terminal Co. jointly with the Baltimore & Ohio Railroad and the City of Cincinnati. The viaduct is 3,500 feet long, 2,800 feet of double-deck construction.

Water consumption estimated to amount to 550,000,000 gallons per year.

225,000 lbs. live steam per hour is the capacity of Boiler House.

8,500,000 kilowatt hours of purchased electrical energy will be used annually, equivalent to the residential needs of a city of over 60,000 population.

The station can accommodate, daily, 17,000 people and 216 trains — 108 in — 108 out.

Main concourse (rotunda) dome has a span of 180 feet and a clear height of 106 feet.

Train concourse is 450 feet long and 80 feet wide.

Eight station platforms extend 1,600 feet.

ROBT. A. TAFT
GEN. COUNSEL—DIRECTOR
(Taft, Stettinius & Hollister)

A. WORCESTER
PRESIDENT
(ired V. P.—N. Y. C. Lines)

E. H. BANKER
SECRETARY
(Exec. Asst. to V.P. & G.M.—N.Y.C.R.R.)

C. W. GALLOWAY
DIRECTOR
(V. P.—B. & O. R. R.)

H. E. NEWCOMET
DIRECTOR
(V. P.—Penn. R. R.)

J. B. MUNSON
DIRECTOR
(V. P.—C. N. O. & T. P. Rwy.)

OFFICERS AND DIRECTORS THE CINCINNATI

C. S. MILLARD
CHRMN. BOARD OF MGRS.
(V. P. and Gen. Mgr.—N. Y. C. R. R.)

GEO. D. CRABBS
VICE-PRES. AND DIRECTOR
(Pres.—Philip Carey Mfg. Co.)

WM. COOPER PROCTER
DIRECTOR
(Chrmn. Brd.—Procter & Gamble Co.)

J. E. CRAWFORD
DIRECTOR
(Gen. Mgr.—N. & W. Rwy.)

G. D. BROOKE
DIRECTOR
(V. P. and Gen. Mgr.—C. & O. Rwy.)

T. E. BROOKS
DIRECTOR
(V. P.—L. & N. R. R.)

UNION TERMINAL COMPANY   MARCH 31, 1933

RUSSELL WILSON
MAYOR

C. A. DYKSTRA
CITY MANAGER

MEREDITH YEATMAN
FINANCE COMMITTEE

CHARLES O. ROSE
CHAIRMAN, FINANCE COMMITTEE

JULIAN A. POLLAK
FINANCE COMMITTEE

JOHN D. ELLIS
CITY SOLICITOR

L. B. BLAKEMORE
CLERK OF COUNCIL

OFFICIALS OF THE CITY OF CINCINNATI

J. E. ROOT
SERVICE DIRECTOR

MYRON DOWNS
CITY PLANNING COM'N ENG'R

ALFRED BETTMAN
CHRMN. CITY PLANNING COM.

IRWIN M. KROHN
PRESIDENT, PARK BOARD

H. H. KRANZ
HIGHWAY ENGINEER

C. M. STEGNER
BUILDING COMMISSIONER

AT THE TIME OF DEDICATION MARCH 31, 1933

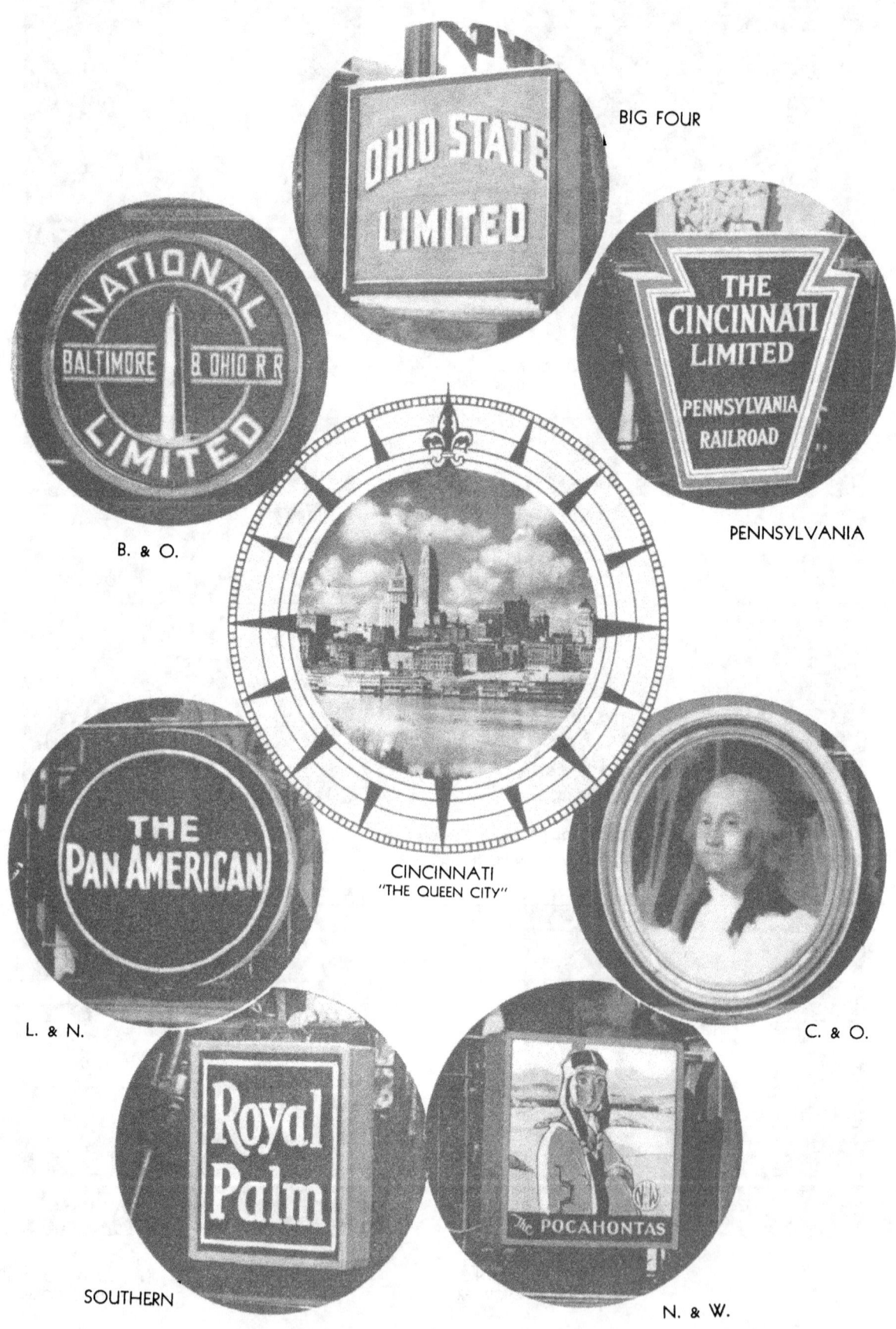

CINCINNATI
UNION TERMINAL

AMERICAN Railroad development is a fascinating story. It would require much time and wide research to assemble the materials of that story; and then, having these in hand, a compelling unfoldment of the epic would involve creative imagination.

Transportation, particularly transportation by rail, plays the leading role in the development of agriculture, industry and commerce. It is obviously the vital thing in the growth of cities. Cities untouched and avoided by railroad lines are doomed. They can never grow.

By virtue of a central location as between the Atlantic Seaboard and the Mississippi Valley and the remoter West; and, further, in view of the fact that the city seemed to be the destined gate-way to the South, Cincinnati early was entered by a railroad. Presently by another, and on to the proud day when she could boast of seven trunk lines.

These seven railroads used five separate passenger terminals. This arrangement was awkward, inconvenient, embarrassing. Other cities of far less importance, industrially and commercially, were building union terminal stations; but Cincinnati only talked about her terminal station to be — and the years ran on.

Definitely, two things had to be accomplished before Cincinnati could ever acquire a unified, centralized freight and passenger terminal. First the idea must be sold to the railroads entering the city, and, after that, the prospect of such a consummation must be brought home to the people.

What Cincinnati needed was a leader to sell her union terminal project — a man who could confront and silence objectors by valid argument and convincing figures, a man who could inspire city-wide confidence in the feasibility and worthwhileness of this great development.

Fortunately for Cincinnati, George Dent Crabbs, a citizen whom the city delights to honor, was available for this important work and appeared to have been molded for this gigantic task. President of one of Cincinnati's oldest and largest manufacturing companies — The Philip Carey Company — Director of the Fourth District Federal Reserve Bank, director of numerous other commercial organizations, and one to whom the community has always turned for advice and counsel in civic enterprises, George Dent Crabbs became the man of the hour.

Mr. Crabbs, at great personal sacrifice, undertook the burden of securing a terminal for Cincinnati with the same tact, patience, perseverance, fairness and keen business judgment that characterized his Chairmanship of Cincinnati's Community Chest, his splendid war work and his every day business life. George Dent Crabbs is indeed the modern Cincinnatus coordinating the desires of seven separate railroads into one unified front, and giving to the City of Cincinnati a landmark that for practicability and beauty is unsurpassed in this country.

Cincinnati's Union Terminal will ever stand as a monument to four years of untiring effort on the part of this leading citizen. It is fitting that the visitors who will come and go, as well as all citizens of Cincinnati pay tribute to this splendid achievement of George Dent Crabbs.

The new Terminal brings the passenger service of all the railroads entering and serving the City together at a site conveniently situated less than one mile from the planned civic center of the near future.

The intersection of Central Parkway and Laurel Street is at the center of a circle which, with a radius of 1¼ miles, sweeps along the north bank of the Ohio River along Front Street for the whole distance between the Louisville and Nashville and the Cincinnati Southern, Ohio

River bridges. Included within this circle, which also touches the west bank of Millcreek, are all five of the vanishing veteran railroad passenger stations; the beautiful Inwood, Lincoln and Eden Parks as well as Redland Field.

Within a circle of one mile radius from the same center are found the new Court House, the Post Office on Government Square, the Dixie Terminal, City Hall, and the new Cincinnati Union Terminal.

The City and the Terminal Company are to be congratulated on the opportunity afforded by hearty cooperation, to provide as fine an architectural placement for a structure of this character as can be found in the United States.

Having, as it were, taken a bird's eye view of the new Terminal in relation to the City and the participating railroads, it is now in order to make a more detailed inspection of Terminal Building itself to the end that it be not judged unworthy of the important place it must now fill in the life of the City.

From Music Hall westward the approach to the Terminal is along Laurel Street widened and improved by the City itself into what has, in these days, come to be known as a super-highway.

Freeman Avenue, an important north-south thoroughfare at the east end of Lincoln Park, is soon reached. From here the reconstructed Park engages the attention. The laudable decision of the City to reconstruct this park as a part of, and in harmony with, the vehicular approach to the new station has resulted in the creation of one of the finest approaches to a public or semi-public building to be found in America.

The spacious Plaza is the result of much care and thought in all stages of the project. Its size has permitted the individual provision for each type of vehicle used in serving the station traffic. Buses, taxicabs, and private cars have all received separate treatment. The traffic to and from the station is therefore highly segregated and orderly in consequence.

In recognition of the fact that the lake which had been a part of Lincoln Park was necessarily omitted in its reconstruction, in harmony with its use in part as the station approach, a subaqueously illuminated combination of a fountain, cascade and pool which otherwise might have been too elaborate, was provided in the center of the foreground of the Plaza where the general grade is still upward toward the entrance level.

The mass of the building standing at the top of this rising and tastefully embellished slope is compelling and substantial. Its outline is symmetrical and pleasing and the design is to say the least unusual. The keynote of its development was that it was created to meet, in a complete and satisfactory way, all of the practical and complicated requirements of a modern union terminal passenger station in a community of about three-quarters of a million population.

As the Station satisfied such a typical need of this machine age, it was considered inappropriate to attempt a design after the classic styles, as has been so generally done with railroad stations in the past. Simplicity of form and composition, economy and taste in the application of materials and convenience and compactness in arrangement, were the guiding principles throughout.

The observer is now prepared to enter this imposing structure. Whether the entrance is made from private cars through the main Plaza level portal or from cabs and buses via the several tunnels and their means of access to side entrances and exits on the main concourse floor, the result is substantially the same. One arrives in the large open semi-circular main concourse, whose diameter is 180 feet, and under the semi-dome, far above, whose outside base diameter is 200 feet. The clear height from the floor to the finished interior at the center is 106 feet.

The large free open space under this exceptionally large semi-dome is unusually impressive, and creates in the observer a distinct sensation of vastness.

As to the interior, all architectural embellishment was achieved by the use of materials of appropriate texture and color. There is little to

be found anywhere which is reminiscent of the classic orders of architecture. The elements of texture and color of material are combined tastefully to secure dignified, restful and pleasing effects.

The patterns woven into the terrazzo floor were made as helpful as possible in guiding the traveler between the principal features. In the concourse waiting room over the tracks, instead of the formal wooden benches, use was made of soft leather covered settees and chairs arranged in informal groups, reserving space for circulation and access to the train gates.

An even more intimate note is struck in the men's and women's shops and in the barber shop. In the treatment of the news reel theatre auditorium where travelers may seek entertainment, and in the various booths, shops and concessions, including the restaurant and lunch room, a more radical departure from the usual decorative embellishments and furnishings is observable. Each was designed, built and completely furnished with different effects, but, nevertheless, in harmony with the whole general conception. This, rather than leave parts to the taste or whim of concessionaires. Advanced ideas in merchandising were provided for and individuality and intimacy in each section in harmony with the whole were earnestly sought.

The resulting treatment of the stairways and ramps to the train platforms and the sheltering canopies, is noticeably brighter and more pleasing than the usual uninteresting treatment accorded to these features.

In the absence of the usual architectural embellishments such as columns, mouldings and pilasters, certain of the prominent surfaces in the important interior spaces required some special treatment. Mosaics were in general used for this purpose as the most suitable, durable and easily maintained. These are reproduced and described in detail in the earlier part of this book.

The train concourse waiting room is in the rear of the building, its long axis coinciding with the axis of the Plaza in front, extended westerly through the center of the station building.

After leaving the main concourse and passing through the checking lobby one enters this large and imposing enclosed space some 450 feet long and 80 feet wide. It is directly over the station tracks and platforms below. Along either side are stairs and ramps to the various train platforms. At the end near the main concourse is found the conductor's visa. Nearby are the train announcement boards, news stand and soda fountain.

There are eight platforms with sixteen tracks below the waiting room concourse, with provision for the addition of six more tracks in the future.

The baggage space is below the main floor level alongside and at the level of the tracks. Arrangements are made for baggage trucks to reach the baggage room via Dalton Street, which passes underneath the Plaza, thus at no time interfering with the vehicular traffic on the Plaza itself.

The structural work to the rear of the dome is extended above the main concourse level several stories in height. This space is arranged as office space for the Terminal Company staff and other services including dispatcher's office, signal and telephone equipment.

In the equipment of the restaurant, lunch room and kitchen, care has been taken to make use of the most modern, sanitary and durable materials and appliances. The completed equipment includes refrigeration, incinerator, bakery, automatic dishwashers, and meat shop.

In a building as large as the Station and as complex in its functioning, the mechanical equipment is necessarily important as well as complicated. In general, however, without going into detailed description of the whole installation, it can be said that full advantage has been taken of the best that the present state of the arts has provided in the various and sundry technical branches.

The steam for heating purposes for the Station and auxiliary needs is furnished from a central boiler house located over a mile away from the Station building.

One-half of the air supplied to the train concourse is fresh air from the outside, heated to room temperature and released through grilles in the combination ceiling lighting fixtures. The other half is taken from the room itself and after being passed through fully covered fan driven heating units where the air is heated sufficiently to balance the heat loss, it is then discharged through a grille downward on the inside of the doors.

The news reel theatre is supplied with cooled air during summer use.

The electric current for lighting and power is supplied by the local power company to the building switchboard over two separate high tension lines, to avoid as far as possible any outside breakdown in the service.

The main concourse half dome is illuminated by lamps controlled by dimmers and concealed in coves in the ceiling surface. The Plaza facade is floodlighted from lighting units installed on island standards in the Plaza some distance from the building. The main jets of the Plaza fountain are illuminated by colored floodlights.

The design and construction of the building, as well as of all other features of the Terminal improvements, were under the supervision of Col. Henry M. Waite, Chief Engineer for the Cincinnati Union Terminal Company. Alfred Fellheimer-Steward Wagner, New York, were the architects for the passenger station proper and its platforms and platform canopies. Paul Cret, Architect, Philadelphia, acted as architectural critic and adviser as to the exterior ensemble of the building.

Winold Reiss prepared the cartoons from which the wall mosaics were executed. Jean Bourdelle was responsible for the painted murals and ceilings, as well as the carved lacquered linoleum decorative panels. Maxfield Keck prepared the models and supervised the stone carvings for the exterior. The general contractor was James Stewart and Company, Inc., New York.